THE MILLERS REST IN PEACE

THE MILLERS REST IN PEACE

DESCENDANTS OF JOHN GEORGE MILLER
(JOHANN GEORG MÜLLER)

CAROL J. BELL

Genealogy House
Amherst, Massachusetts

The Millers Rest in Peace, copyright 2018 by Carol J. Bell

First published 2018

Genealogy House Publishers
a division of White River Press
PO Box 3561
Amherst, MA 01004
Genealogyhouse.net

ISBN: 978-1-887043-37-3

Book design credit:
Douglas Lufkin
Lufkin Graphic Designs
www.LufkinGraphics.com

Photo credits:
Cover, frontispiece, end page photographs were taken by the author in 2013 and 2015 at Greenwood Cemetery, Wheeling, West Virginia. Shown is the MILLER gravesite with the large monument marking plots W323 and W325. Other photos used by permission.

Sources:
The Wheeling Intelligencer, Wheeling, WV; *The Intelligencer*, Wheeling, WV; *The Wheeling Register*, Wheeling, WV; *Wheeling News-Register*, Wheeling, WV; *The Hopewell News*, Hopewell, VA; West Virginia Archives and History, Division of Culture and History, Charleston, WV; Ohio Department of Health, Division of Vital Statistics, Columbus, OH; Clerk's Office, Ohio County Court, Wheeling, WV; Ohio County Public Library, Wheeling, WV

Obituaries were transcribed by Carol Bell in the original style of the day, exactly as they were published. Obituaries were not found for John George Miller, Metta Wagener Miller, and Christian Ernest Miller. Short comments were written by Carol Bell for these three people.

Library of Congress Cataloging-in-Publication Data

Names: Bell, Carol J., 1946- author.
Title: The Millers rest in peace : descendants of John George Miller (Johann
   Georg Müller) / Carol J. Bell.
Other titles: Descendants of John George Miller (Johann Georg Müller)
Description: Amherst, Massachusetts : Genealogy House Publishers, [2018]
Identifiers: LCCN 2017058630 | ISBN 9781887043373 (cloth : alk. paper)
Subjects: LCSH: Wheeling (W. Va.)--Genealogy. | Miller, John George,
   1831-1914--Family. | Miller family. | Mueller family. | Wheeling (W. Va.)--Biography.
Classification: LCC F249.W5 B45 2018 | DDC 929.20973--dc23
LC record available at https://lccn.loc.gov/2017058630

DEDICATION

In loving memory of the two longest-living descendants of John George Miller: my mother, Elizabeth Miller Bell, the best mom in the world, and my aunt, Doris Miller Cooper.

Acknowledgements

I am grateful to Miller descendants Elizabeth Miller Bell, Doris Miller Cooper, Rebecca Miller Szabo, Linda Maruca Zeik, Phyllis Maruca Barnhart, Elizabeth Kabala Smith, and also Judy Burkhart Miller, wife of Christian E. Miller, and Elizabeth Stephens Dorsch, a Morris descendant, for sharing memories and photographs of our ancestors. Each of you is special to me, and I thank you for your help. A thank you also goes to John Bowman for granting permission to use the steamboat photograph from his book, *Wheeling: The Birthplace of the American Steamboat,* and to Jim Otte for his photograph of the Red Men Cemetery.

Dear Ancestor

Your tombstone stands among the rest;
Neglected and alone,
The name and date are chiseled out
On polished, marbled stone.
It reaches out to all who care,
It is too late to mourn,
You did not know that I exist,
You died and I was born.
Yet each of us are cells of you
In flesh, in blood, in bone,
Our blood contracts and beats a pulse
Entirely not our own.
Dear Ancestor, the place you filled
One hundred years ago
Spreads out among the ones you left
Who would have loved you so.
I wonder if you lived and loved,
I wonder if you knew
That someday I would find this spot,
And come to visit you.

—Unknown

Contents

Miller Descendants

BIOGRAPHIES

THE MILLERS REST IN PEACE

Descendant List
of John George Miller

1-John George MILLER (16 Oct 1831-25 Mar 1914)

+Metta A. C. WAGENER (8 Mar 1835-29 Oct 1886)

..... 2-Mene MILLER (25 Apr 1857-27 Apr 1857)

..... 2-Christian Ernest MILLER (Dec 1861-1901)

..... +Amanda Elizabeth HEINLEIN (22 Jan 1871-23 Jun 1929)

.... 3-Harry Andrew MILLER (1 Jul 1889-8 Apr 1951)

.... +Laura May WEISHAR (29 Mar 1890-23 Mar 1928)

.... 4-Doris Katherine MILLER (5 Jul 1915-9 Feb 2016)

.... 4-Emma Elizabeth "Libby" MILLER (3 Jun 1918-23 Sep 2014)

.... 4-Helen Virginia MILLER (31 Jul 1919-17 May 1991)

.... 4-Laura Mae "Lauramae" MILLER (2 Aug 1922-26 Apr 2003)

.... 4-Harry Andrew "Bud" MILLER Jr. (13 Jul 1927-5 Jun 1968)

.... +Virginia E. DAUGHERTY (13 Nov 1903-13 May 1958)

.... 3-Minnie Metta MILLER (14 Sep 1891-27 Sep 1952)

.... +Lawrence William FURLONG (5 Sep 1891-17 Mar 1961)

.... 4-Edna Elizabeth FURLONG (24 Mar 1919-16 Jul 1969)

.... 3-Female MILLER (5 Feb 1894-7 Feb 1894)

.... 3-John Mortimer MILLER (31 Jan 1895-6 Aug 1974)

.... +Myrtle Mae WARD (8 Jan 1898-7 Aug 1976)

.... 3-George Edward "Whitey" MILLER (2 Sep 1897-4 Apr 1965)

.... +Bertha Leona PRICE (21 Nov 1900-24 Dec 1972)

.... 4-Edna Elloween MILLER (16 Oct 1917-23 Dec 1989)

.... 4-Evaline Ruth "Evelyn" MILLER (19 Oct 1919-30 Aug 1920)

INTRODUCTION

John George Miller (Johann Georg Müller) of Germany (Prussia) and Metta Wagener of Germany (Hannover) immigrated to the United States in the mid-nineteenth century, a time when many Germans were leaving their homeland for a better life. They met after they came to America and were married in Ritchietown (South Wheeling), Virginia in 1856. Many of their descendants have found Greenwood Cemetery, Wheeling, West Virginia, their last resting place.

In 1914, John George Miller, the patriarch of this strong German family, became the first member of our Miller family to be buried at Greenwood Cemetery in Wheeling, West Virginia. Other Ohio Valley area cemeteries chosen by our Miller families were Mount Calvary Cemetery, Red Men Cemetery, Holly Memorial Gardens, Riverview Cemetery, and Greenwood Cemetery (formerly Rose Hill Cemetery), Bellaire, Ohio.

In an effort to preserve a piece of our Miller family history in one collection, this book presents obituaries and information about John George Miller and the first three generations of his descendants. Regardless of where they lived, most "came home" to be buried in Wheeling area cemeteries. A brief description of each cemetery is also provided.

Spanning over 160 years in America from my second great-grandfather John George Miller to my nephews, Douglas Bell and Derek Bell, there have been six generations of Millers in my direct line. I am proud to be a Miller descendant.

Carol J. Bell
2018

God has given us no greater blessing than that of belonging to a loving and loyal family—and it will be so, always and forever.

—Richard L. Evans

Cemeteries

Greenwood Cemetery, Wheeling, WV

Greenwood Cemetery is located along National Road next to the Dimmeydale neighborhood of Wheeling. The cemetery was incorporated in March 1866. Its grounds have expanded to nearly 100 acres. More than 40,000 people are buried there. It is the final resting place of many of Wheeling's most influential citizens.

Mount Calvary Cemetery, Wheeling, WV

Mount Calvary Cemetery is located along National Road adjacent to Wheeling Park and is locally referred to as the "Catholic Cemetery." The original cemetery consisted of 32 acres. It has expanded over the years to 200 acres, with 80 acres developed. More than 41,800 people are buried there. The first interment was made in September 1872.

Photograph courtesy of Jim Otte.

Red Men Cemetery, Wheeling, WV

Red Men Cemetery is located on a slope above Center Wheeling. In 1862, members of the Red Men Order purchased seven acres for a cemetery for their families. The Order of Red Men is America's oldest fraternal organization founded in 1765 and originally known as the Sons of Liberty. This is an old abandoned burial ground, long neglected and overgrown.

Holly Memorial Gardens, Colerain, OH

Holly Memorial Gardens is located along U.S. Route 250 near Colerain. The cemetery was founded in 1959 and has 49 developed acres.

Riverview Cemetery, Martins Ferry, OH

Riverview Cemetery is located along North 8th Street in Martins Ferry. It is a very large cemetery of 155 acres, with almost 100 acres developed, and dates back to pre-Civil War days. It has nearly 50,000 interments. This cemetery is very hilly, with a paved driveway circling through it. A fantastic view of the Ohio River and the valley is seen from the top.

Greenwood Cemetery, Bellaire, OH

Greenwood Cemetery is located along State Route 214 near Bellaire. It was founded in 1859. A large cemetery of 42 acres, it was originally named Rose Hill Cemetery.

MILLER DESCENDANTS
WHO LIVED A VERY SHORT TIME OR ARE STILL LIVING

Mene Miller*	25 Apr 1857–27 Apr 1857	Daughter of John George and Metta Miller
John Miller*	circa 1869–Death?	Son of John George and Metta Miller. Lived to be at least age 11; no more records found.
Edna Miller*	circa 1874–Death?	Daughter of John George and Metta Miller. Lived to be at least age 6; no more records found.
Female Miller*	5 Feb 1894–7 Feb 1894	Daughter of Christian and Amanda Miller
Infant Miller*	Birth/Death before 1900	Child of Christian and Amanda Miller
Evaline Miller	19 Oct 1919–30 Aug 1920	Daughter of George Edward and Leona Miller. Cause of death was whooping cough; buried at Rose Hill (Greenwood) Cemetery, Bellaire, OH.
Anna Miller	7 Apr 1921–23 Oct 1921	Daughter of George Edward and Leona Miller. Cause of death was gastroenteritis; buried at Rose Hill (Greenwood) Cemetery, Bellaire, OH.
Carl Ackermann	8 Oct 1946–9 Oct 1946	2nd Son of George and Josephine Miller Ackermann. Cause of death was premature birth; buried at Mount Calvary Cemetery, Wheeling, WV.
David Ackermann	Born 1948–Living	3rd Son of George and Josephine Miller Ackermann. Living in Wheeling, WV, area.
Michael Ackermann	Born 1952–Living	4th Son of George and Josephine Miller Ackermann. Living in Wheeling, WV, area.

*Burial location unknown

Miller Descendants

JOHN GEORGE MILLER

b. 16-Oct-1831   d. 25-Mar-1914   age 82

cause of death   arteriosclerosis

buried in Greenwood Cemetery, Wheeling

No obituary was found. About John George Miller: He emigrated from Germany (Prussia). In 1856, he married Metta Wagener in South Wheeling, Virginia (now West Virginia), and they became the parents of six children. He was buried in an unmarked grave at Greenwood Cemetery, Section S, Lot 60, Wheeling, West Virginia. Find more information about him on page 88.

Greenwood Cemetery, Section S, Lot 60. Note the tombstone with peonies growing in front. The unmarked graves of John George Miller; his daughter, Emma Miller Meyer Suter; and her second husband, John Suter, are in the large open space to the right of that tombstone.

METTA WAGENER MILLER

b. 8-Mar-1835   d. 29-Oct-1886   age   51

cause of death   no record found

buried in Red Men Cemetery, Wheeling

No obituary was found. About Metta Wagener Miller: She emigrated from Germany (Hannover). In 1856, she married John George Miller in South Wheeling, Virginia (now West Virginia), and they became the parents of six children. She was buried in Red Men Cemetery, Wheeling. Find more information about her on page 88.

Red Men Cemetery is neglected and overgrown.

Photograph courtesy of Jim Otte.

CHRISTIAN ERNEST MILLER

b. Dec-1861   d. 1901   age   40

cause of death   no record found

buried in Greenwood Cemetery, Wheeling

No obituary was found. About Christian Ernest Miller: He was born in 1861 in Virginia (now West Virginia). In 1887, he married Amanda Elizabeth Heinlein of Bellaire, Ohio, and they became the parents of six children, two of whom died in infancy. Christian died in 1901 at age 40, leaving Amanda with four small children. He was buried at Rose Hill (now Greenwood) Cemetery, Bellaire. Many years later, his remains were transferred to the Miller gravesite in Greenwood Cemetery, Wheeling, West Virginia. Find more information about him on page 90.

Wheeling's Old North Market on a typical Saturday morning. This photo was taken in 1901, the same year that Christian Miller died. Note the horse-drawn wagons. Photograph from *Landmarks of Old Wheeling* (published in 1943).

AMANDA ELIZABETH HEINLEIN MILLER MORRIS

b. 22-Jan-1871   d. 23-Jun-1929   age   58

cause of death   brain hemorrhage (stroke)

buried in Greenwood Cemetery, Wheeling

Mrs. Morris Dies Suddenly, Well-Known South Side Resident
Passes Sunday Night

Mrs. Amanda Morris, 58, wife of Robert A. Morris and well-known resident of South Wheeling, died suddenly last night at 6:30 o'clock at the family home, 2847 Eoff street. Mrs. Morris had partaken of her evening meal with the rest of the members of her family and had gone to her bedroom when she collapsed. Death was said to have been due to a sudden heart attack. Mrs. Morris was a former member of the German Methodist church. Besides her husband she leaves the following sons and daughters: Harry A. Miller, of Triadelphia; Mrs. Lawrence Furlong, of Wheeling; John M. Miller, of Wheeling; George Edward Miller, of Detroit; Robert C. Morris, of Wheeling; Mrs. Louis Stephens, of Wheeling; Mrs. Fred Herrick, of Detroit; Arthur J. Morris, at home. The following step-sons and daughters also survive: Archibald A. Morris, of Wheeling; Nile G. Morris, of Wheeling; Mrs. George Poehner, of Albany, Cal.; Randall Morris, at home. One sister, Mrs. Joseph Mayhugh, of Bellaire, one brother, Christian Heinlein, of Triadelphia, and 23 grandchildren also survive. The body has been removed to the Cooey-Bentz funeral home at 36th and Jacob streets. Services will be held on Wednesday at 2 o'clock in the Cooey-Bentz funeral home. Rev. W.H. Fields, pastor of the First Christian church, will officiate. Interment will be made in Greenwood cemetery.

Wheeling Register, Wheeling, WV, 24 June 1929

Harry Andrew Miller

b. 1-Jul-1889   d. 8-Apr-1951   age 61
cause of death   cirrhosis of liver, esophageal hemorrhage
buried in Greenwood Cemetery, Wheeling

H. A. MILLER
for HOUSE of DELEGATES

Harry Miller, Auto Dealer, Dies Sunday

Harry A. Miller, 61, resident of 117 Fifteenth st., vice-president and general manager of the J.M. Miller Auto company, prominent civic and fraternal leader and the oldest auto dealer in point of service in the city, died last night at 8:30 o'clock in the Ohio Valley General Hospital. A son of the late Christian and Amanda Miller, he was born in Bellaire, Ohio, July 1, 1890. He attended public school in Bellaire, O., Benwood, and Wheeling, attended Elliott Business College and International Correspondence school, Scranton, Pa., of which

school he was district secretary for several years, specializing in the bookkeeping salesmanship and English. His first employment was at the Riverside plant of the National Tube company in Benwood. He entered the auto business at its infancy in 1914. He was one of the incorporators and president of the H. A. Miller Auto company, Steubenville, O., and an incorporator and president and general manager of the Dulaney-Miller Auto company of this city; sales manager of the Elm Grove Motor Co., sole owner of the Miller Auto Trading company of Elm Grove, and was for a

time territory manager of the Autocar company branch of Pittsburgh. Later he and his brother incorporated the J. M. Miller Auto company, located at 23rd and Market sts., with which he was associated at the time of death. He was an attendant at the First English Lutheran church. He was a member of Ohio Lodge No. 1, Ancient Free and Accepted Masons, a Knight Templar and member of the Wheeling Union Chapter, Royal Arch Masons. He was a member of the Wheeling Automobile Association, and the United States Coast Guard auxiliary. He had traveled extensively in Europe. Surviving are his wife, Mrs. Virginia Daugherty Miller; two sons, Harry A. Miller, Jr., Wheeling and William Carr Miller, Detroit, Mich., five daughters, Mrs. Doris Cooper, Cleveland, O., Mrs. Lauramae Powers, Long Beach, Calif., Mrs. Elizabeth Bell, Mrs. Helen Klug and Mrs. Eileen Thomas, all of Wheeling. Seven brothers, Edward G. Miller, McMechen; John M., Robert, Randall, Nile, Arch and Arthur Miller, all of Wheeling; four sisters, Mrs. Minnie Furlong, Mrs. Lillian Stephens, Mrs. Virginia Herrick and Mrs. Fay Poehner, all of Wheeling, and 9 grandchildren. Friends are being received at the McCoy funeral home, 44 Fifteenth st. Services will be held in the parlors Wednesday, at 2:30 p.m. The Rev. Charles G. Aurand, pastor of the First English Lutheran church will officiate. Interment will be in Greenwood cemetery.

Wheeling News-Register, Wheeling, WV
9 April 1951

LAURA MAY WEISHAR MILLER

b. 29-Mar-1890   d. 23-Mar-1928   age   37

cause of death   tuberculosis

buried in Greenwood Cemetery, Wheeling

Mrs. Harry A. Miller Dies, Elm Grove Woman Passes After Month's Illness of Complications

     Mrs. Laura May Miller, 37, wife of Harry A. Miller and a resident of Wheeling her entire life, died at 5 o'clock Friday evening at her home on Union hill near Elm Grove following a month's illness of complications. Born in Wheeling, the decedent had resided her entire life here and was widely known. She was a member of the First English Lutheran church of Wheeling and of the Zelta Cook Sunday school class. She is survived by her husband, manager of the Miller Auto Trading company at Elm Grove, four daughters, Doris, Elizabeth, Helen and Laura, and one son, Harry A. Miller, Jr. Her father and mother, Mr. and Mrs. Joseph J. Weishar, of Union Hill, one brother, Joseph D. Weishar of Fulton, and one sister, Mrs. W.M. Morgan of Wheeling, also survive. The body was removed to the Crider funeral home at Elm Grove where it was held pending the completion of funeral arrangements. Services will be conducted Monday afternoon at

2 o'clock at the place of death. Rev. Charles G. Aurand, pastor of the First English Lutheran church, will have charge of the services and interment will occur in Greenwood cemetery.

Wheeling Register, Wheeling, WV
24 March 1928

DORIS KATHERINE MILLER COOPER

b. 5-Jul-1915   d. 9-Feb-2016   age   100

cause of death   cardiac arrest

buried in Greenwood Cemetery, Wheeling

Doris Katherine Cooper, a 48-year resident of Prairie Village, KS, died on February 9, 2016, at the age of 100. She was born on July 5, 1915, in Wheeling, WV, the daughter of Harry Andrew Miller and the former Laura May Weishar. She graduated from Triadelphia High School, Class of 1934, where she met her husband, George Warrick Cooper. They were married in 1936 and had two children. The family lived in Elm Grove, WI, for 14 years where they enjoyed boating on Lake Michigan. After moving to the Kansas City area, George and Doris enjoyed many more years of boating on Lake of the Ozarks in central MO, and spending time at their cottage on the lake. Doris was a faithful member of a Bible-believing Christian church until late in life, when her hearing impairment prevented her from hearing the sermons. Doris had a long life, interspersed with much happiness and sorrow. She had faith in her Lord and Savior Jesus until the end. She was preceded in death by her husband, George Sr.; her daughter, Martha Beth Armbruster; her brother, Harry A. (Bud) Miller Jr.; and three sisters, Elizabeth (Libby) Bell, Helen Klug, and Lauramae Powers. She is survived by her son, George (Ann) Warrick Cooper Jr. of Cottage Grove, WI; three grandchildren, Patty Finley of Overland Park, KS, Rebecca Cardarella of Cottage Grove, WI, and Amy Hazlewood of Mt. Horeb, WI; three great grandchildren, Jase Finley, Bradley Hazlewood, and Elise

Hazlewood; and many nieces and nephews. Friends will be received at Kepner Funeral Home, 166 Kruger St, Wheeling, WV on Wednesday, February 17, 2016, from 6-8 p.m. where services will be held on Thursday, February 18, 2016, at 11 a.m. with Pastor Paul Schaeffer officiating. Interment will follow in Greenwood Cemetery, Wheeling, WV. Personal condolences can be expressed at www. kepnerfuneral. com. "For me to live is Christ, to die is gain."

Wheeling News-Register, Wheeling, WV
16 February 2016

EMMA ELIZABETH MILLER BELL

b. 3-Jun-1918   d. 23-Sep-2014   age   96

cause of death   cerebrovascular accident (stroke)

buried in Greenwood Cemetery, Wheeling

BELL, Elizabeth "Libby" Miller, 96, of Wheeling, WV, died Tuesday, September 23, 2014, at Wheeling Hospital. She had lived at the Altenheim Home, 1387 National Road, Wheeling, WV, for 14 years and spent the last couple of months at Beacon House Assisted Living in St. Clairsville, OH. Libby was born, June 3, 1918, in Wheeling, the second daughter of the late Harry A. Miller, Sr. and Laura May Weishar Miller. Her birth name was Emma Elizabeth; she was named after her two grandmothers. Libby was a devoted wife, mother, grandmother, and friend. She came of age during the Great Depression, was a graduate of Triadelphia High

School Class of 1936, and during WWII was among the women of the Greatest Generation working on the home front at Wheeling Stamping Company. She was a retired employee of the business office at Ohio Valley Medical Center and the oldest active member of Roney's Point United Presbyterian Church, Triadelphia, where she had served on several committees. Libby was a member of the Order of the Eastern Star (O.E.S.) for over 70 years. She was initiated in 1942, Past Worthy Matron of Liberty Chapter No. 51, and a member of Bethany

Chapter No. 64. She was also a former member of the Jean Laupp Thomas Circle of the International Order of the King's Daughters and Sons. She was known for her kindness and fun-loving spirit. She enjoyed travel and had been coast to coast in the U.S. and on several trips to Europe. She was also known by many as a lady who loved using her hands for sewing and crafting. This was evidenced by the clothing, crocheted blankets, needle point, and latch hook items she made. Her many pieces of work are family treasures. In addition to her parents, she was preceded in death by her husband, Willard Downing Bell in 1979, whom she married July 20, 1940; her grandparents, Joseph and Emma Forsch Weishar and Christian and Amanda Heinlein Miller; a brother, Harry A. Miller, Jr.; and two sisters, Helen Klug and Lauramae Powers. She will be forever loved by her daughter, Carol J. Bell of Atlanta, Georgia.; a son, Daniel W. Bell and his wife Debra of Wheeling; two grandsons, Douglas I. Bell and Derek R. Bell, both of Wheeling; a sister, Doris Cooper of Prairie Village, Kansas, cousins, and many nieces and nephews. Friends will be received on Tuesday, September 30, 2014 from 2-4 and 6-8 p.m. at Kepner Funeral Home, 166 Kruger Street, Elm Grove, Wheeling (304-242-2311), where the funeral service will be held Wednesday, October 1, 2014 at 11 a.m. with The Reverend Darrin Jones officiating. Interment will be in Greenwood Cemetery, Wheeling. In lieu of flowers, memorial donations in Libby's name may be made to Roney's Point United Presbyterian Church, 169 Dallas Pike, Triadelphia, WV, 26059. Online condolences may be offered to the family at www.kepnerfuneral.com.

Wheeling News-Register, Wheeling, WV
28 September 2014

Miller siblings in 1956: Doris, Bud, Lauramae, Helen, and Libby.

Helen Virginia Miller Klug

b. 31-Jul-1919   d. 17-May-1991   age 71

cause of death   lung cancer

buried in Mount Calvary Cemetery, Wheeling

KLUG, Helen V. Miller, 71, of Millcreek Place, Kissimmee, Fla., formerly of Wheeling, died Friday in Humana Hospital, Kissimmee. She was a member of St. Michael Catholic Church, Wheeling. Surviving are her husband, Charles J.; a son, Michael D. of Wheeling; a daughter, Mrs. Douglas (Chris) Ernest of Kissimmee; three sisters, Libby Bell of Wheeling, Doris Cooper of Prairie Village, Kan., and Lauramae Powers of Anaheim, Calif; three grandchildren. Friends received 2-4 and 7-9 p.m. Tuesday and Wednesday at Altmeyer Funeral Home, 154

Kruger St., Elm Grove, Wheeling. Mass of Christian Burial will be celebrated at 1 p.m. Thursday in St. Michael's Catholic Church, Wheeling. Interment in Mount Calvary Cemetery, Wheeling.

The Intelligencer, Wheeling, WV
18 May 1991

LAURAMAE MILLER POWERS

b. 2-Aug-1922   d. 26-Apr-2003   age 80

cause of death   lung cancer

buried in Greenwood Cemetery, Wheeling

LAURAMAE MILLER POWERS, 80, formerly of Wheeling, WV, died Saturday, April 26, 2003, in Lakewood, Calif. She was born August 2, 1922, in Triadelphia, WV, a daughter of the late Harry A. and Laura May Weishar Miller. She was a 1940 graduate of Triadelphia High School and a 1943 graduate of Wheeling Hospital School of Nursing; a retired RN having worked at St. Mary's Hospital, Long Beach, Calif, and Lakewood Regional Medical Center, Lakewood; an Army Nurse, Second Lieutenant during World War II; and a former member of the First English Lutheran Church, Wheeling. In addition to her parents, she was preceded in death by her husband, David L. Powers in 1979, whom she married April 2, 1946, her grandparents, Joseph John and Emma Weishar; a brother, Harry A. Miller Jr., a sister, Helen Klug; two grandchildren, Michael David and Joshua Andrew Copeland; a great-grandchild, Jonathan Christopher Angdahl; and an aunt and uncle, Clerk of Ohio County Court Raymond Falland and his wife Bertha. Surviving are two daughters, Joyce Copeland and her husband, Randy, of Lakewood, Calif. and Janice Towner of Garden Grove, Calif.; two sisters, Doris Cooper of Kansas and Elizabeth Bell of Wheeling; three grandchildren, Aaron Towner, Sandi Lee Angdahl and Jeremy Daniel Copeland; four great-grandchildren, Jeff, Jenni, Curt and Chris Angdahl;

and several nieces and nephews. Friends received 2-4 and 6-8 p.m. Monday at Altmeyer Funeral Home, 154 Kruger Street, Elm Grove, Wheeling where services will be held at 10 a.m. Tuesday, May 6, 2003 with Pastor David Twedt officiating. Military graveside services will be held in Greenwood Cemetery, Wheeling with her grandson Jeremy Copeland, Air Force (ROTC) participating in graveside services.

Wheeling News-Register, Wheeling, WV, 4 May 2003

LAURAMAE POWERS
2ND LT US ARMY
WORLD WAR II
AUG 2 1922 ✝ APR 26 2003
BELOVED DAISY   R N

LAURAMAE POWERS
1922   2003
BELOVED MOM & GRANNY

HARRY ANDREW MILLER JR.

b. 13-Jul-1927   d. 5-Jun-1968   age 40

cause of death   kidney cancer

buried in Greenwood Cemetery, Wheeling

MILLER, Harry A., Jr., 40, of Anaheim, Calif., formerly of Wheeling, died Wednesday in the Long Beach Memorial Hospital, Long Beach, Calif., following a long illness. He was born in Wheeling, July 13, 1927 the son of Harry A. and Laura May Weishar Miller, Sr. He was a Protestant by Faith, and an electrician by trade. He was a member of the Nelson Lodge, No. 30, AF and AM in Wheeling. He was a U.S. Navy veteran, serving in WWII. Survivors include his wife, Donalda Layton Miller; two daughters, Mrs. Linda Szczypiorski, of Fullerton, Calif., and Cheryl Dawn, of the home; one son, Harry A., III, of the home; four sisters, Mrs. Doris K. Cooper of Prairie Village, Kan., Mrs. Elizabeth M. Bell, Valley Grove, W.Va., Mrs. Helen V. Klug, Wheeling, Mrs. Lauramae Powers, of Lakewood, Calif.; one maternal

U. S. S. NORTH CAROLINA

aunt, Mrs. Raymond J. Falland, of Wheeling. Friends may call at the Kepner Funeral Home, National Road and Bethany Pike, 12-3 and 7-9 p.m. Sunday. Services will be held at the funeral home at 1 p.m., Monday with the Rev. John S. Streng officiating. Interment in Greenwood Cemetery. Nelson Lodge, No. 30, AF and AM will hold graveside services.

The Intelligencer, Wheeling, WV

8 June 1968

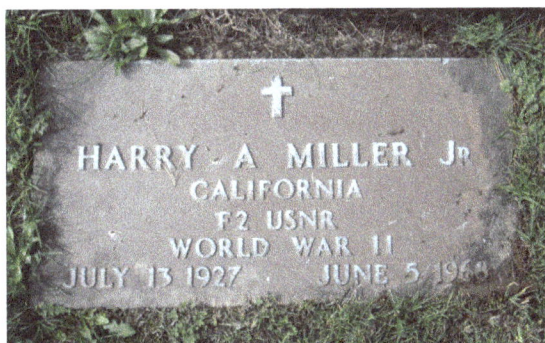

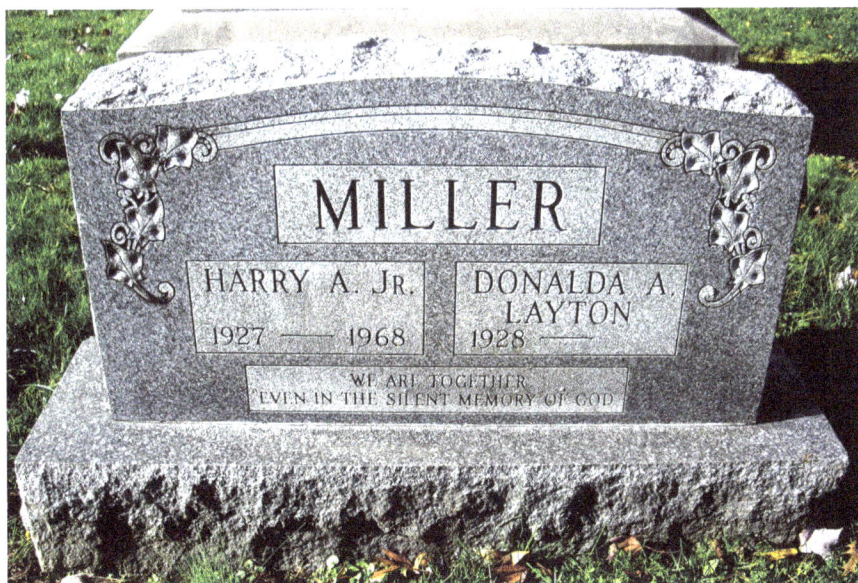

Virginia E. Daugherty Carr Miller

b. 13-Nov-1903   d. 13-May-1958   age 54

cause of death   ruptured brain aneurysm

buried in Greenwood Cemetery, Wheeling

Miller, Mrs. Virginia Daugherty, 54, of 93 New Jersey St., died at 4:50 a.m. today in the Ohio Valley General Hospital, where she had been a patient for the past week. Born in Wheeling, Nov. 13, 1903, she was a daughter of Nelson and Dora Cole Daugherty. She had operated the New Island Florist Shop for the past 14 months. She was a Methodist, and was a member of the Iris Court No. 1, Ladies Oriental Shrine, in which she was a member of the Patrol; a member of the Wardah Husam Temple No. 53, Daughters of the Nile; a member of the White Rose Sisterhood, Dames of Malta. Her husband, Harry A. Miller, died in 1951. Surviving are a son, William Carr of Cleveland, O.; a daughter, Mrs. Ivor G. Thomas of Wheeling; a sister, Mrs. William Behrens of Weirton; and four grandchildren. Friends may call at the McCoy Funeral Home, 44 Fifteenth St., where services will be held at 2 p.m. Thursday with the Rev. M.S. Risinger in charge. Interment will be in Greenwood Cemetery.

Wheeling News-Register, Wheeling, WV
13 May 1958

MINNIE METTA MILLER FURLONG

b. 14-Sep-1891   d. 27-Sep-1952   age 61

cause of death   pulmonary embolism

buried in Greenwood Cemetery, Wheeling

Mrs. Minnie Miller Furlong, 61, died at 9:25 p.m. Saturday at the Ohio Valley General hospital after an illness of two weeks. She was born September 14, 1891, a daughter of the late Christian E. and Amanda E. Heinlein Miller. She is survived by her husband, Lawrence W. Furlong; one son, James, at home, one daughter, Mrs. Michael Kabala, of Wheeling; six brothers, J.M. Miller of Bethlehem, George E. Miller, Robert E. Morris, Arthur Morris, Arch E. Morris and Nile G. Morris, all of Wheeling, three sisters, Mrs. Lillian Henke and Mrs. Fred Herrick, both of Wheeling, and Mrs. Fay Poehner, Berkeley, Cal., and three grandchildren. The body was removed to the Beiswenger funeral home, 3828 Jacob st., where friends will be received today. Services in chapel Tuesday at 2:30 p.m. Friends respectfully invited to attend. Interment in Greenwood Cemetery.

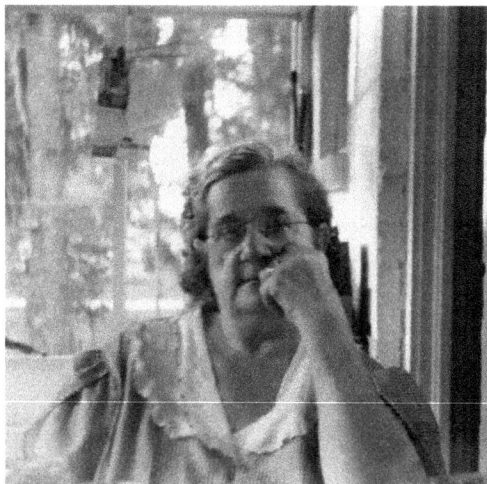

Wheeling News-Register, Wheeling, WV
28 September 1952

Sample of Minnie's handwriting

LAWRENCE WILLIAM FURLONG

b. 5-Sep-1891   d. 17-Mar-1961   age 69

cause of death   coronary occlusion

buried in Greenwood Cemetery, Wheeling

FURLONG, Lawrence William, 69, of 1034 Lind St. and formerly of 4324 Lane H., died at 10:30 a.m. Friday in Wheeling Hospital. He had been ill four months. He was born in Boston Sept. 5, 1891 and was a son of Michael and Elizabeth Furlong. He was an employee of the Wheeling Tile Co., retiring in 1959. A Roman Catholic, he attended St. Joseph's Cathedral. He was married to Minnie Miller Furlong who died in 1952. Surviving are one daughter, Mrs. Edna Kabala of Wheeling; one son, James Schrader of Wheeling; one brother, John P. Furlong of Cleveland; five grandchildren and three great-grandchildren. Friends received at the Beiswenger Funeral Home, 3828 Jacob St. There will be a High Mass of Requiem at 10 a.m. Monday in St. Joseph's Cathedral followed by interment in Greenwood Cemetery. Members of the parish will pray the Rosary at 8 p.m. Sunday at Beiswenger's.

The Intelligencer, Wheeling, WV
18 March 1961

EDNA ELIZABETH FURLONG KABALA

b. 24-Mar-1919   d. 16-Jul-1969   age   50

cause of death   coronary occlusion

buried in Greenwood Cemetery, Wheeling

   KABALA, Mrs. Edna E., 50, 3924 Wood St., died Wednesday at 1 a.m. at Ohio Valley General Hospital. She was born March 24, 1919, in Wheeling, daughter of Lawrence and Minnie Miller Furlong. She was a member of the Immaculate Conception. Surviving are her husband, Michael, three sons, Lance Cpl. Lawrence Michael, Cherry Point, N.C., Michael Joseph and John, both at home; a daughter, Mrs. Ronald (Elizabeth) Smith, Bethlehem; a brother, James Schrader, Mozart; six grandchildren. Friends may call at Beiswenger Funeral Home, 3828 Jacob St., after 7:30 p.m. today. High Mass of Requiem Friday at 9 a.m. at Immaculate Conception Church, with Fr. Joseph A. Bell as celebrant.

Wheeling News-Register, Wheeling, WV
16 July 1969

1927

JOHN MORTIMER MILLER

b. 31-Jan-1895   d. 6-Aug-1974   age   79

cause of death   cause of death confidential by Florida law

buried in Greenwood Cemetery, Wheeling

J.M. Miller Succumbs In Florida

John M. Miller, former owner and operator of the J.M. Miller Auto Company in Wheeling for 35 years, died Tuesday in Sarasota Memorial Hospital, Sarasota, Fla. A resident of 1051 Myrtle St., Sarasota, Fla., formerly of Bethlehem, Miller was born in Bellaire, O. on Jan 21, 1895, son of Christian and Amanda Miller. He was 79 years of age. He was a member of the First Christian Church, Wheeling; the Ohio Lodge No. 1, AF and AM; Scottish Rite Bodies; 32nd degree KCCH; Osiris Temple of the Shrine; Wheeling Post No. 1 of the American Legion and the 80th division of the Veterans Association. Surviving are his widow, Myrtle Ward Miller; one daughter, Mrs. Anna McGehee of Wheeling; one brother, Arthur Morris of Wheeling; one sister, Mrs. George Poehner of California. Friends received at the McCoy Funeral Home, 44 Fifteenth St., Wheeling, 7-9 p.m. Thursday and 2-4 and 7-9 p.m. Friday. Funeral services will be held Saturday at 10

a.m. at the First Christian Church with the Rev. Thomas G. Kerns officiating and Dr. Hubert L. Barnett in charge. Interment in Greenwood Cemetery, Wheeling.

Wheeling News-Register, Wheeling, WV

7 August 1974

MYRTLE MAE WARD CONN MILLER

b. 8-Jan-1898   d. 7-Aug-1976   age   78

cause of death   cardiac arrest

buried in Greenwood Cemetery, Wheeling

MILLER, Myrtle Ward, 78, of 1051 Myrtle St., Sarasota, Fla., formerly of Wheeling, died Saturday in Ohio Valley General Hospital. She was a member of the First Christian Church of Wheeling. She was preceded in death by her husband, John M. Miller, in 1974. Surviving are a daughter, Mrs. Anna L. McGehee of Wheeling, and several nieces and nephews. Friends received at the McCoy Funeral Home, 44 Fifteenth St., Wheeling, on Sunday from 12-3 and 7-9 p.m. and on Monday from 2-4 and 7-9 p.m. Services will be held at the First Christian Church on Tuesday at 10:30 a.m. Interment in Greenwood Cemetery.

Wheeling News-Register, Wheeling, WV
8 August 1976

John and Myrtle Miller

GEORGE EDWARD MILLER

b. 2-Sep-1897   d. 4-Apr-1965   age   67

cause of death   cancer of esophagus

buried in Holly Memorial Gardens, Colerain, OH

Miller, George E., of 21 Forty-eighth St., Wheeling, died at 3:30 a.m. Sunday in the Ohio Valley General Hospital. He had been ailing for several months. Born Sept. 2, 1897, in Bellaire, he was the son of Christian E. and Amanda Heinlein Miller. A member of the First Christian Church, he was a retired driver for the Delta Concrete Co. Surviving are his wife, Bertha L. Price Miller; two sons, John and Christian both of Martins Ferry; two daughters, Mrs. Philip Maruca of Wheeling and Mrs. Don Lyons of Fort Pierce, Fla.; five brothers, John Miller of Sarasota, Fla., and Wheeling; Robert, Arthur, Arch and Nile Morris of Wheeling; two sisters, Mrs. Lillian Heitz of Wheeling and Mrs. Fay Poehner of Berkeley, Calif.; and 11 grandchildren. Friends may call at the Altmeyer Funeral Home, 1400 Eoff St., where services will be held at 2 p.m. Wednesday with Rev. Hubert Barnett officiating. Interment will be in Holly Memorial Gardens.

Wheeling News-Register, Wheeling, WV
5 April 1965

REGISTRATION CARD   a
SERIAL NUMBER 5290   ORDER NUMBER 1553

BERTHA LEONA PRICE MILLER

b. 21-Nov-1900   d. 24-Dec-1972   age 72

cause of death   cardiac arrest

buried in Holly Memorial Gardens, Colerain, OH

MILLER, Mrs. Bertha (Leona), 72, 520 S. Huron St., died Sunday, at West Palm Beach, Fla. She was born Nov. 21, 1900 at Belington, W.Va., daughter of Charles B. and Delila Ann Price. She was a member of St. Paul's United Church of Christ. She was preceded in death by her husband, George Edward in 1965. Surviving are two sons, John, Martins Ferry; Christian, Wheeling; two daughters, Mrs. Phillip (Edna) Maruca, Wheeling; Mrs. Donald (Barbara) Lyons, West Palm Beach, Fla.; two sisters, Mrs. Iva Sturm, Moundsville; Mrs. Dorothy Furbee, Portsmouth, Va.; 11 grandchildren, six great grandchildren. Friends received at Altmeyer Funeral Home, 1400 Eoff St., Wednesday 2-4, 7-9 p.m., where services will be held Thursday at 2 p.m. with the Rev. Robert Coupe officiating. Interment in Holly Memorial Gardens.

The Intelligencer, Wheeling, WV
27 December 1972

EDNA ELLOWEEN MILLER MARUCA

b. 16-Oct-1917   d. 23-Dec-1989   age 72

cause of death   respiratory failure, pneumonia

buried in Greenwood Cemetery, Wheeling

MARUCA, Edna E. Miller, 72, of 309 S. Front St., Wheeling Island, died Saturday in Ohio Valley Medical Center, Wheeling. She was a retired employee of the former Cinemette Corp., Wheeling, and a member of St. Paul United Church of Christ, Wheeling. She was a member of the Island Youth Center, Island Community Association, Girl Scouts of America and Nika-Mary Martha Class of St. Paul United Church of Christ. She was preceded by her husband, Philip B., on Jan. 1, 1981. Surviving are three daughters, Mrs. Robert (Gloria) Shoemaker of Sewickley, Pa., Mrs. Terry (Linda) Zeik of Wexford, Pa., and Phyllis J. Maruca Barnhart of Charleston; two brothers, John E. Miller of St. Clairsville and Chris E. Miller of Mozart; a sister, Barbara Lyons of Prince George, Va.; three grandchildren, Travis, Bethany, and Todd Zeik. Friends received 7-9 p.m. Monday, and 2-4 and 7-9 p.m. Tuesday at Altmeyer Funeral Home, 1400 Eoff St., Wheeling. Services will be held at 1 p.m. Wednesday at St. Paul United Church of Christ, Wheeling, with the Rev. Robert A. Coupe Jr. officiating. Interment in Greenwood Cemetery, Wheeling.

Wheeling News-Register, Wheeling, WV
24 December 1989

EDNA E. MARUCA

1917   1989

JOHN EDWARD MILLER

b. 22-Jul-1923   d. 4-Oct-2007   age   84

cause of death   chronic obstructive pulmonary disease

buried in Riverview Cemetery, Martins Ferry, OH

MILLER, John E., 84, of Martins Ferry, Ohio, died Thursday, October 4, 2007, in East Ohio Regional Hospital, Martins Ferry, after a long illness. He was born July 22, 1923 in McMechen, W.Va., a son of the late George Edward and Leona Miller. Mr. Miller was also preceded in death by two sisters, Edna Maruca and Barbara Lyons; and his beloved dachshund, Heidi. Mr. Miller retired after 20 years with Prudential Insurance as an agent and a manager. He began his career in retail and worked over 20 years as a buyer for the former Hub Department Store of Wheeling. He was an avid Mountaineer fan and was hopeful he could get to a WVU game this fall. He was a longtime member of St. Paul's Episcopal Church and had served on the Vestry. Surviving are his devoted wife of 62 years, Mary Lou Miller; one daughter and son-in-law, Becky and Steve Szabo, Follansbee, W.Va.; a son, John Eighme Miller and his wife, Denise, North East, Pa.; a brother and sister-in-law, Chris and Judy Miller, Wheeling, W.Va.; six grandchildren, Tracey (Chris) Welch, Follansbee, Susan (Jeff) Bergman, Canton, Ga., Stephanie (Joe) Sampson, Hermitage, Tenn., Jon Duffy Miller, North East, Becky (Joe) Repko, Perrysburg, Ohio, and Zane Miller, North East; two great

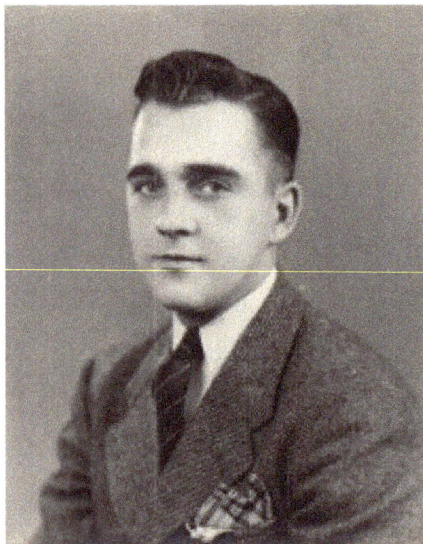

grandchildren, Kelaen and Olivia Welch and Baby Bergman, due in 2008; and many nieces and nephews including Gloria Shoemaker, Linda Zeik, Phyllis Barnhart, Laurie Pollock, and Christian Miller. Friends will be received from noon-3 and 6-8 p.m. on Sunday, October 7, 2007 at the Heslop Funeral Home, Walnut at Fifth, Martins Ferry. Services will be held at St. Paul's Episcopal Church, 611 Walnut St. on Monday, October 8, 2007 at 11 a.m. with the Rev. John P. Brandenburg officiating. Interment will follow in Riverview Cemetery, Martins Ferry.

The Intelligencer, Wheeling, WV
6 October 2007

BARBARA LEE MILLER WRIGHT MINGER LYONS

b. 4-Jul-1926   d. 9-Jan-1999   age   72

cause of death   Virginia death record becomes public 25 years after event

cremated

Barbara Lee Lyons, 717 Cabin Creek Road, Hopewell, departed this life Saturday, Jan. 9, at John Randolph Medical Center. She was a native a Wheeling, W.Va., and daughter of the late George and Leona Price Miller, and widow of Donald Lyons. She is survived by a son, George E. Wright Sr. (Susan), of Hopewell; three daughters, Debbie Romanyk, of Florida, Mrs. Karen Sixtotos, of Texas, and Janeen Sparks, of Florida; two brothers, John Miller, of Ohio, and Christian Miller, of W.Va.; 15 grandchildren; 10 great grandchildren and other relatives and friends. A memorial service will take place at 7 p.m. Thursday at the Greater Faith Vineyard Christian Fellowship, Crater Road, Petersburg, with Pastor Charles E. Crocker officiating. Arrangements entrusted to the staff of Turner-Bland Funeral Home in Hopewell.

The Hopewell News, Hopewell, VA
12 January 1999

A footnote: Barbara Miller Lyons was cremated in Virginia. No burial information was found.

Large monument at the Miller gravesite in Greenwood Cemetery, Wheeling, WV

CHRISTIAN ERNEST MILLER

b. 31-Jan-1942   d. 29-Jan-2011   age   68

cause of death   metastatic colon cancer

buried in Mount Calvary Cemetery, Wheeling

Miller, Christian E. (Ernie), 68, of Mozart Meadows, Wheeling, died peacefully Saturday, January 29, 2011. He was born January, 31, 1942, in Glen Dale WV, son of the late George E. and Bertha Leona Price Miller. Chris was the President and owner of Chris Miller Furniture in Wheeling since 1979, and a member of the Cathedral of St. Joseph and Our Lady of Peace Catholic Church both in Wheeling. He was a member of the Wheeling Country Club where he was past president, a board member of the former Wheeling National Bank, a member of the F.O. P. A., the Saints and Sinners, the Round Table Stock Club, a member and past president of Gyro International, a member of the Cave Club, the PAP Club, and the IOLA Club. He was past president of the former Wheeling Development Corp., a former board member of the Wheeling Area Chamber of Commerce, past president of the Wheeling High School Boosters, and a Fourth Degree Knights of Columbus. Chris was an avid golfer and a proud member of the 2005 Wheeling Country Club Member-Member championship team. He was also a loyal WVU and Steelers Fan. Chris was a loving husband, father and grandfather and enjoyed his many close friends. He always said he loved his 3G's in life: God, Grandchildren, and Golf. He will be sadly missed by all who knew and loved him. In addition to his parents, he was preceded in death by 4 sisters and 1 brother. He is survived by his wife, Judy Burkhart Miller, a son, Christian M. Miller and his wife Tammy of Wheeling, a daughter, Laurie L. Pollock and her husband Chris, of Eighty-Four Pa.,

4 grandchildren, C. J. Miller, Joshua Miller, Carlie Pollock, and Hailey Pollock, his sister-in-law, Mary Lou Miller, his aunt, Dorothy Price McDowell, and many nieces and nephews. Friends will be received on Monday, January 31, 2011, from 2-8 p.m., at the Kepner Funeral Home, National Road at Bethany Pike, Wheeling. Friends then received on Tuesday, February 1, 2011 at the Cathedral of St. Joseph, 1300 Eoff St., Wheeling, from 9:30-10:30 a.m. Mass of Christian Burial will be celebrated at 10:30 a.m. with Monsignor Kevin Quirk and Father Dennis Scheulkens officiating. Entombment in Mount Calvary Cemetery Mausoleum, Wheeling. Memorial contributions may be made in lieu of flowers to the Cathedral of St. Joseph, 1300 Eoff St., Wheeling, or to Our Lady of Peace Catholic Church, Mount Olivet, Wheeling. Friends may offer condolences to the family at www.kepnerfuneral.com.

Wheeling News-Register, Wheeling, WV
30 January 2011

EMMA LOUISA MILLER MEYER SUTER

b. Jul-1865   d. 1-Aug-1928   age   63

cause of death   bowel cancer

buried in Greenwood Cemetery, Wheeling

Suters Services

Funeral services for Mrs. Emma Suter, McMechen resident, who died Wednesday night while visiting with relatives at Roneys Point, will be conducted at the home of her brother, Otto A. Miller, 2420 Marshall street, Benwood. Interment will be made in Greenwood cemetery.

Wheeling Register, Wheeling, WV
3 August 1928

A footnote: Emma Suter lived at the County Home in Roney's Point, West Virginia, for the last 10 months of her life.

Greenwood Cemetery, Section S, Lot 60. Note the tombstone with peonies growing in front. In the large open space to the right of that tombstone are the unmarked graves of John George Miller; his daughter, Emma Miller Meyer Suter; and her second husband, John Suter.

JOHN MEYER

b. Dec-1857   d. 15-Jul-1910   age   52

cause of death   no record found

buried in Greenwood Cemetery, Wheeling

Meyer Funeral

      The funeral of the late John Meyer, who died Friday at his home in the First ward, will take place this afternoon. Services will be conducted at the house at 2 o'clock, following the interment will take place at Greenwood cemetery. The deceased was 53 years of age and is survived by a wife but no children.

Wheeling Register, Wheeling, WV
17 July 1910

      A footnote: John Meyer emigrated from Germany in 1882 and was a laborer in a glue factory in 1910. He died in his 53rd year.

JOHN WEST SUTER

b. 18-Mar-1858   d. 28-Mar-1925   age   67

cause of death   chronic myocarditis

buried in Greenwood Cemetery, Wheeling

Death Summons Old Riverman, John W. Suter Dies at His Home on South Side at 74

John W. Suter, 74, veteran riverman, died at 11:45 o'clock last night at his home, 4017 Wood street, after an illness of four months, due to heart trouble. Mr. Suter was born in Hannibal, Ohio. He was a member of steamboat crews for many years and spent the greater part of his life on the river. A few years ago he had settled in Wheeling and married Emma Miller. He is survived by his wife, two sisters and a brother. Funeral services will be held at his home here with burial in Greenwood cemetery.

Wheeling Register, Wheeling, WV
29 March 1925

A footnote: Based on the birth date listed on John Suter's death record, he died at age 67 not age 74.

Photograph courtesy of John Bowman.

Greenwood Cemetery, Section S, Lot 60. Note the tombstone with peonies growing in front. In the large open space to the right of that tombstone are the unmarked graves of John George Miller; his daughter, Emma Miller Meyer Suter; and her second husband, John Suter.

OTTO ADOLPH MILLER

b. 12-Dec-1876   d. 10-Sep-1969   age   92

cause of death   stroke

buried in Greenwood Cemetery, Wheeling

Miller, Otto A., 92, 21 Carole Ave., Glen Dale, died Wednesday at 10:45 p.m. at Reynolds Memorial Hospital, Glen Dale. He was born Dec. 12, 1876, in Bellaire, a son of George and Metta Miller. He was a retired carpenter and contractor; member of the Church of God, McMechen; member of Knights of Pythias. His wife, Annie Miller Miller, died in 1947. Surviving are two daughters, Margaret, at home; Mrs. George A. (Josephine) Ackermann, Wheeling; three grandchildren; a nephew. Friends may call at Altmeyer Funeral Home, 1400 Eoff St. today and tomorrow 2-4, 7-9 p.m. Services in the chapel there Saturday at 11 a.m. with the Rev. Ernest Hall officiating. Interment in Greenwood Cemetery.

Wheeling News-Register, Wheeling, WV

11 September 1969

ANNA MARGARET MILLER MILLER

b. 24-Mar-1876   d. 27-Jul-1947   age 71

cause of death   arteriosclerotic heart disease

buried in Greenwood Cemetery, Wheeling

Mrs. Miller of McMechen Dies Sunday

    Mrs. Anna M. Miller, 71, wife of Otto A. Miller and a resident of McMechen for the past 42 years, died Sunday morning at 8:20 o'clock in the Ohio Valley General hospital. In ill health for the past two and a half years, Mrs. Miller had been a patient in the hospital for six days. She was born in Wheeling, March 24, 1876, a daughter of the late Valentine and Josephine Dole Miller, and was educated in St. Alphonsus school. Married at Benwood on August 1, 1899, to Otto A. Miller, Mrs. Miller had been a resident of McMechen since 1905. The family home is situated at 2420 Marshall street. The deceased was a member of St. James church, McMechen, and belonged to Review No. 38, Women's Benefit Association. Surviving are her husband, Otto A. Miller; two daughters, Miss Margaret E. Miller, at home; Mrs. George Ackermann of Wheeling; five sisters, Miss Mary Miller, Mrs. Elizabeth Burke, Mrs. Ida Haberfield, all of Benwood; Mrs. Theresa Polton of Akron, Ohio; Mrs. Isadore F. Poulton of Wheeling, and one grandson, Russell Ackermann, Wheeling. Another sister, Mrs. Emma B. Bernhart, died July 1 of this year. Friends are being received in the Altmeyer funeral home where brief services to be held Wednesday morning at 8:15 o'clock will be followed by a High Mass of Requiem at 9 o'clock in St. Alphonsus church. The Rev. Joseph J. Daly, pastor of St. James church, McMechen, will be the celebrant of the Mass. Greenwood cemetery will be the place of burial.

The Wheeling Intelligencer, Wheeling, WV, 28 July 1947

Margaret Elizabeth Miller

b. 30-Mar-1900   d. 15-Jun-1973   age 73

cause of death   acute myocardial infarction

buried in Greenwood Cemetery, Wheeling

MILLER, Miss Margaret E., 73, of 21 Carole Ave., Glen Dale, W.Va. died Friday at 9 p.m. at the Reynolds Memorial Hospital. She was born in Benwood, W.Va., March 30, 1900, daughter of the late Otto A. and Anna Miller. She was a member of the St. Jude Church, Glen Dale, school principal of the Marshall County school system, serving at Center School, Benwood; to King in McMechen; Park View, Moundsville and Glen Dale Grade School. She was a member of the Alpha Delta Kappa Sorority of Moundsville, the National Retired Teachers Association and the McMechen Women's Club. She is survived by one sister, Mrs. George (Josephine) Ackermann of Wheeling, three nephews, two great-nieces and two great-nephews. Friends received at Altmeyer Funeral Home, 1400 Eoff St., Sunday and Monday 2-4 and 7-9 p.m. Mass of Christian Burial on Tuesday at 10:30 a.m. at St. Alphonsus Church in Wheeling. Interment in Greenwood Cemetery. Rosary Devotions Monday at 8 p.m.

Wheeling News-Register, Wheeling, WV
17 June 1973

JOSEPHINE MARY MILLER ACKERMANN

b. 12-Jun-1914   d. 12-May-1980   age 65
cause of death   cardiac arrest
buried in Greenwood Cemetery, Wheeling

ACKERMANN, Josephine M. Miller, 65, of 21 Carole Ave., Glen Dale, formerly of South Wheeling, died Monday in Reynolds Memorial Hospital, Glen Dale. She was a member of St. Alphonsus Catholic Church, Wheeling. She was preceded in death by her husband, George A. Ackermann in 1977. Surviving are three sons, Michael of Warwood, David of Wheeling, and Russell of Idaho Falls, Idaho; six grandchildren. Friends received at the Altmeyer Funeral Home, 1400 Eoff St., Wheeling, 2-4 and 7-9 p.m. Wednesday and Thursday. Interment in Greenwood Cemetery. Rosary devotions at 7:30 p.m. Thursday.

The Intelligencer, Wheeling, WV
13 May 1980

A footnote: Josephine Ackermann's birth year, as listed in the Social Security Death Index, was 1914. Her tombstone shows 1916.

ACKERMANN

GEORGE A.
1920 — 1977

JOSEPHINE M.
1916 — 1980

George Andrew Ackermann

b. 30-Jan-1920   d. 12-Mar-1977   age   57

cause of death   cardiac standstill

buried in Greenwood Cemetery, Wheeling

ACKERMANN, George A., 57, of 21 Carole Ave., Glen Dale, died Saturday at the Reynolds Memorial Hospital, Glen Dale. He was a member of the St. Alphonsus Catholic Church and an employee of the International Harvester Corp. in Shadyside. He was a veteran of the United States Navy in World War II. He was a member of the Fourth Degree Knights of Columbus — Carroll Council, B.P.O.E. 28, the Cave Club and the American Legion. Surviving are his wife, Josephine Miller Ackermann; three sons, George Russell of Idaho Falls, Idaho, David E. of Cincinnati, Ohio, and Michael J. of Charleroi, Pa.; one brother, Cyril J. Ackermann of Wheeling; five grandchildren. Friends received at the Altmeyer Funeral Home, 1400 Eoff St., Wheeling, Monday and Tuesday, 2-4 and 7-9 p.m. Mass of Christian burial Wednesday at 11 a.m. in St. Alphonsus Church. Interment in Greenwood Cemetery. Knights of Columbus rosary devotions Tuesday at 7:30 p.m.

The Intelligencer, Wheeling, WV

14 March 1977

ACKERMANN

GEORGE A.
1920 — 1977

JOSEPHINE M.
1916 — 1980

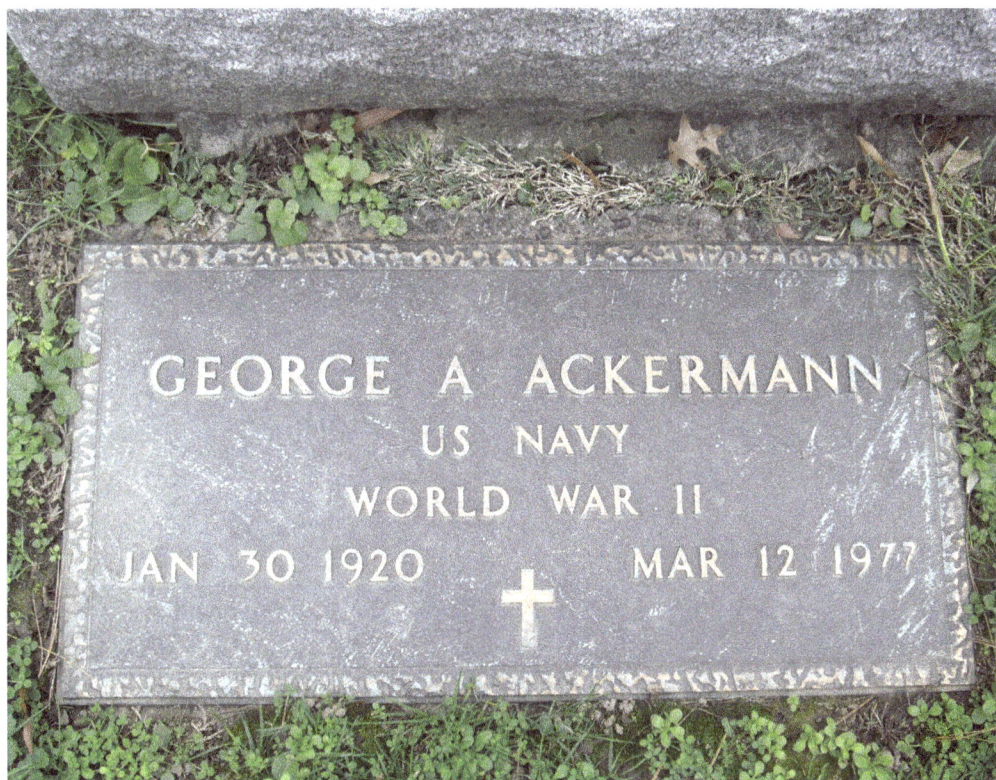

GEORGE A ACKERMANN
US NAVY
WORLD WAR II
JAN 30 1920   MAR 12 1977

George Russell Ackermann

b. 30-May-1942   d. 13-Dec-2009   age 67
cause of death   cause of death confidential by Florida law
buried in Mount Calvary Cemetery, Wheeling

ACKERMANN, George Russell "Russ", 67, died Sunday, Dec. 13, 2009, at his home in Stuart, FL with support by Treasure Coast Hospice, Crisis Care Unit.

He resided in Stuart for the past 13 years, moving from Idaho Falls, ID in April 1996. He was born May 30, 1942 in Wheeling, WV, the eldest son of George Andrew and Josephine Mary (Miller) Ackermann (both deceased). He attended parochial schools in Wheeling, graduating from Central Catholic High School in 1960. He received a B.S. in physics in 1964 from Wheeling College (nka Wheeling Jesuit University) in West Virginia and earned his M.S. in physics in 1972 from Akron University in Ohio. During his education years, he was active in music, tennis, basketball and football, earning a letter in tennis at Wheeling College. Russ served his country as a member of the U.S. Navy during the Vietnam War era, enlisting Nov. 8, 1965. He attended basic training at Great Lakes Naval Training Center, educated at various "A" schools (including a position as trumpeter with the U.S. Navy Band at Memphis, TN) and then transferred to Patrol Squadron Four (VP-4) at Barbers' Point, HI as an Aviation Anti-Submarine Warfare Operator (AW3). He participated in two deployments to Iwakuni, Japan with adjunct service in Vietnam, Taiwan and the Philippines. He was honorably discharged on Nov. 3, 1969 at Long Beach Naval Shipyard in California and was decorated with the Armed Forces Expeditionary Medal

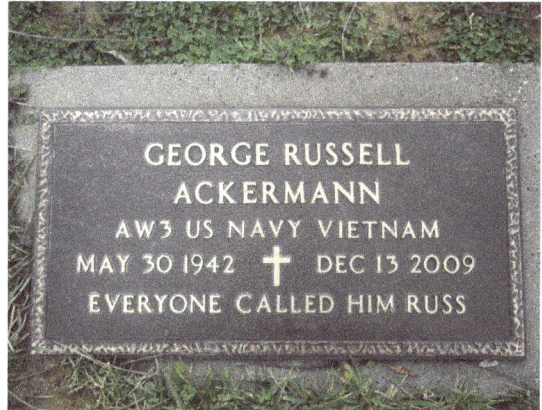

(Korea), the National Defense Service Medal and the Vietnam Service Medal with one bronze star. After his discharge in 1969, he returned to Wheeling with a new wife and three stepchildren. He was primarily employed as a tire engineer with General Tire in Akron, OH; followed by a career as a software designer in Enka, NC; a mathematician with NOAA in Idaho Falls, ID; and a mathematician/

computer specialist for Perot Industries (headquartered in Plano, TX). He was an accomplished musician, a Ham Radio Operator (with the certification of "Extra") and participated as emergency coordinator for the Martin County ARES/RACES group. Russ was dedicated to "giving back." This was evidenced by his adjunct professorship at Indian River State College (IRSC). Because of his love of airplanes and dreams of someday becoming a pilot, he undertook private pilots' training and accomplished the difficult task of passing his "solo" flight. He was a member of the Miles Grant Country Club and the Stuart-Jensen Beach Elks Lodge #1870 of Stuart. In his retirement years, he was first trumpet of the Stuart Community Band, an avid golfer and loved playing tennis. Survivors include his wife of 40 years, Arlene L. (Brown) Ackermann of Stuart; three stepchildren, Mrs. David P. Godin (Karen A. Buchholz) of Glastonbury, CT, Robert E. Buchholz (Nancy) of Omaha, NE and Ms. Trudy E. Buchholz of Stuart; two brothers, David E. Ackermann of Wheeling and Michael J. Ackermann Sr. (Bonnie) of Bellaire, OH; several nieces and nephews; eight step-grandchildren; and two step-great-grandsons. Friends are invited to attend the Mass of Christian Burial that will be held at 10 am, Monday, January 11, 2010, at the chapel of Mary and Joseph at Wheeling Jesuit University, Wheeling, with Rev. James O'Brien, S.J. as celebrant. A private family burial will follow at Mount Calvary Cemetery, Wheeling. The family requests no flowers. Memorial contributions may be made to Treasure Coast Hospice, Crisis Care Unit, 1201 SE Indian St., Stuart, FL 34997.

Obituary Archive, Altmeyer Funeral Homes (http://www.altmeyer.com), George Russell "Russ" Ackermann, died 13 December 2009, accessed November 2015.

BIOGRAPHIES

Adapted from "The Miller Family Tree" Newsletter
Researched and Written by Carol J. Bell

Harry Andrew Miller

Harry Andrew Miller was my grandfather. He was born July 1, 1889, in Bellaire, Ohio, the first son of Christian Ernest Miller and Amanda Elizabeth Heinlein Miller, and the first grandchild of our immigrant ancestor, John George Miller (Johann Georg Müller) of Germany. The earliest known record of Harry is in the 1900 U.S. Census where he was listed as ten-year-old "Ira Andrew." No one knows what the story is behind the "Ira" and "Harry" first names. It is possible that the census enumerator did not understand what was said, thus reporting the wrong name.

He completed the eleventh grade and attended the Elliott Business College and the International Correspondence Schools of Scranton, Pennsylvania, where he specialized in bookkeeping and salesmanship. His first employment was at the Riverside plant of the National Tube Company (pipe mill) at Benwood, West Virginia; in 1914, he entered the auto business when it was in its infancy.

Harry's colleagues said of him: "Although still young in years, he is old in experience." This comment was well earned over the many years he served in various positions as president, general manager, territory manager, or owner of H. A. Miller Auto Company, Dulaney-Miller Auto Company, Elm Grove Auto Company, Miller Auto Trading Company, and Autocar Company. He was also the "Jeffery Man" in the Wheeling district. The Jeffery car was one of the classiest on the market. The brand transitioned several times and eventually became the Jeep-Eagle Division of Chrysler. Later, Harry and his brother John M. Miller incorporated the J. M. Miller Auto Company where Harry was vice president and general manager at the time of his death.

Harry married Laura May Weishar on June 14, 1914. They became the parents of five children: Doris, Elizabeth, Helen, Lauramae, and Harry (Bud) Andrew Jr. The family lived in East Wheeling for a while and worshiped at the nearby First English Lutheran Church. Later they moved to a hilltop farm in Triadelphia to find "fresh air" for Harry's wife, Laura, who was suffering from tuberculosis. She died in 1928 at age 37, leaving him with five children.

In 1917 and again in 1942, Harry registered for the World War I and World War II drafts but was not called for duty. He ran as a Democrat for the West Virginia State House of Delegates but lost the election.

Harry was a member of several Masonic organizations, including Ohio Lodge No. 1, Ancient Free and Accepted Masons, Knights Templar, and Wheeling Union Chapter No. 1, Royal Arch Masons. He also played a saxophone in Wheeling's Osiris Shrine Band.

On June 15, 1944, sixteen years after his beloved Laura passed away, he married Virginia Daugherty Carr. Harry died April 8, 1951 in Wheeling at age 61; he was buried in Greenwood Cemetery. When he died, he had been the auto dealer who had served the city for the longest period of time.

Minnie Metta Miller Furlong

Minnie Metta Miller Furlong was Harry and John Miller's only surviving sister. Minnie was born September 14, 1891, in Bellaire, Ohio, the second child and first daughter of Christian Ernest Miller and Amanda Elizabeth Heinlein Miller, and a grandchild of our immigrant ancestor, John George Miller (Johann Georg Müller) of Germany.

Minnie's parents may have followed one of several German naming customs when choosing her name. The first daughter was usually named after the maternal grandmother; however, it seems that Minnie was named after both of her grandmothers, Wilhelmena and Metta.

Sometime between 1897 and 1900, the Miller family moved from Ohio to Benwood, West Virginia. When Minnie was about ten years old, her father died; in June 1902, her mother married Robert Morris. Minnie's formal education stopped at sixth grade. In 1910, at age 19, she and her stepsister, Fay Morris, were employed as decorators of kitchen enamelware products. At the same time, her future husband, Lawrence Furlong, was an operator at an elevator business in Cleveland.

Lawrence William Furlong, son of Michael and Elizabeth Furlong who emigrated in 1888 from Ireland, was born September 15, 1891, in Boston. By 1894, the Furlong family had moved to Cleveland. Almost twenty years later, Lawrence still lived in Cleveland, and Minnie lived in Benwood. Because they were about 150 miles apart, no one knows how the two met; nevertheless, they married May 29, 1913, in Benwood. The couple moved to Cleveland but came home to South Wheeling in the 1920s.

Minnie and Lawrence had a daughter, Edna Elizabeth, and a secret. Edna's daughter, Elizabeth (Liz) Kabala Smith of Wheeling, told me a family story that was known to only a few people. When Liz was a young girl, she walked to Ritchie Elementary School in South Wheeling. She noticed a man watching her and told her parents about him. One day, her father confronted him. The man said he was Jack, the brother of Liz's mother, Edna, and wanted to know how she was doing. This is when Liz learned that her mother had been adopted.

Edna was born March 24, 1919, to a family named Murphy that had nine children and could not take care of their tenth child. Neighbors found her crying and abandoned in a chicken coop. They asked Minnie and Lawrence, who were unable to have a child of their own, if they wanted the baby. They adopted the newborn but did not want anyone to know what had happened. Years later, the secret was finally revealed.

Minnie also raised her nephew James Irvin Schrader who was the son of James and Laura Morris Schrader, Minnie's half sister. James Irvin was born June 3, 1936. His mother died when he was only eleven months old; his father had his own problems and disappeared from the family.

In 1952, shortly before she died, Minnie sent a letter to her niece, Doris Miller Cooper, which gives us a carefree personal peek into her life. The letter reported that:

- Minnie's brother, John Miller, paid all the expenses of a two-week trip for her to visit him in Florida. She was grateful and thoroughly enjoyed every minute.
- Her daughter, Edna, suffered severely with poison ivy.
- Minnie had diabetes and was treated with insulin. Edna got too nervous giving her mother insulin injections so she quit, and Minnie gave them to herself.

- Minnie missed her brother Harry (d. April 8, 1951). She wrote: "I have to take a cry every time I think of Harry. I miss him so much. He was so good to me."

After an illness of two weeks, Minnie died at Ohio Valley General Hospital on September 27, 1952. Lawrence retired from his night watchman duties at Wheeling Tile Company in 1959. He died March 17, 1961. Both are buried at the Miller gravesite in Greenwood Cemetery.

John Mortimer Miller

Harry Andrew Miller's brother was my great-uncle, John Mortimer Miller. John was born January 31, 1895, in Bellaire, Ohio, the second son of Christian Ernest Miller and Amanda Elizabeth Heinlein Miller, and a grandchild of our immigrant ancestor, John George Miller (Johann Georg Müller) of Germany.

By the time John was five years old, the Miller family had moved from Ohio to Benwood, West Virginia. He completed eighth grade; in 1910, at age 15, he worked as a switch tender in a steel mill yard. By 1917, he was working as a roughing table operator (tending machines that roll steel) at National Tube Company (pipe mill) in Benwood.

John was described as tall, medium build, gray eyes, and dark brown hair when he registered for the World War I draft in 1917. He was conscripted into the Army and served as a Sergeant in the 80th "Blue Ridge" Division, 314th Field Artillery, Battery "C", which was assigned to the 155th Field Artillery Brigade. Most of the men were from West Virginia. The soldiers of the 80th Division trained at Camp Lee, Virginia. They disembarked in France on June 8, 1918, and were involved in the Meuse-Argonne Battle that took place between the Meuse River and the Argonne Forest in France. Years later, in 1942, John registered for the World War II draft.

After World War I, John planned to marry a lady named Ethel, but she became ill and died. On November 26, 1924, he married Myrtle Mae Ward Conn, a divorcée and mother of one child, Anna L. Conn, who was age 10 at the time of the marriage. According to his niece, John's mother was not happy with the marriage, and there was a fuss in the family for a while over Myrtle. Apparently Myrtle had left her first husband, Kirby Conn, to marry John.

In 1928, brothers John and Harry purchased adjacent burial lots 323 and 325 in Section W of Wheeling's Greenwood Cemetery. A large Miller monument sits at the center among the Miller family graves. The first interment at the site was for Laura Weishar Miller, Harry's wife, who died in 1928.

John lived in the Bethlehem community of Wheeling and was owner of the J. M. Miller Auto Company for thirty-five years. After a long career, he retired to Sarasota, Florida. He was a member of the First Christian Church and belonged to several Masonic organizations, including Ohio Lodge No. 1, Ancient Free and Accepted Masons, Scottish Rite Bodies, 32nd degree Mason, KCCH (Knight Commander of the Court of Honour, a designation to honor men of outstanding ability and commitment), Osiris Temple of the Shrine, Wheeling Post No. 1 of the American Legion, and the 80th Division of the Veterans Association.

John died in Sarasota on August 6, 1974. Two years later, his lovely Myrtle died in Wheeling on August 7, 1976; three years later their daughter, Anna Conn McGehee, died on August 3, 1979. All three of them died in the month of August. They are buried at the Miller gravesite in Greenwood Cemetery.

GEORGE EDWARD MILLER

George Edward Miller was the kid brother of Harry, Minnie, and John. He was called Edward, but because he was towheaded with very light blond hair, his nickname was Whitey. He is remembered by several of his nieces as Uncle Whitey. Edward was born September 2, 1897, in Bellaire, Ohio, the fifth child and youngest son of Christian Ernest Miller and Amanda Elizabeth Heinlein Miller, and a grandchild of our immigrant ancestor, John George Miller (Johann Georg Müller) of Germany. During the nineteenth century, many Germans chose the Ohio River Valley as a favored destination because of jobs and inexpensive land, which often resembled the homeland. In 2010, 11 percent of Wheeling's population was still German, the second largest ethnic group after English.

Sometime between 1897 and 1900, the Miller family moved from Ohio to Benwood, West Virginia, a town that borders the south side of Wheeling. To put the early twentieth-century era in perspective, West Virginia's first telephone exchange was established in Wheeling in 1880 and served 51 telephones; by 1899, only two years after Edward was born, the 1000th telephone was installed. When Edward was about four years old, his father died; in June 1902, his mother married widower Robert Arthur Morris, her next-door neighbor.

Edward's formal education stopped at ninth grade. Edward and his brothers must have had good writing teachers as all the boys had excellent penmanship as noted in various documents they signed.

Edward married Bertha Leona Price of Belington, West Virginia. Because Leona was underage, written consent for marriage was provided by Charles B. Price, her father. The couple was married March 3, 1917, in Benwood by G.F.

Hein, a Lutheran Pastor. Edward's age was listed as 21, but he was actually 19. Leona's age was listed as 17, but she was actually 16.

Edward worked as a furnace man at the Riverside plant of the National Tube Company, one of several companies that eventually merged to form Wheeling Steel. He was employed there when, in 1918, victory over the Germans in World War I was growing closer. He registered for the draft then, but was not called for duty.

Edward and Leona became the parents of six children: Edna Elloween, Evaline (Evelyn) Ruth, Anna Elizabeth, John Edward, Barbara Lee, and Christian Ernest. Sadly, two of their babies died just eight months apart, Evaline at age 10 months and Anna at age 6 months.

The couple had thirteen grandchildren. Several of Edward's grandchildren remember him as a Pittsburgh Pirates' baseball fan, sitting at the kitchen table, listening to a game while enjoying an Iron City beer.

Between 1929 and 1934, the Miller family lived in Detroit, Michigan, where Edward was a driver of an ice wagon, and Leona was a pie maker at a bakery, but by 1934, they were living back home in Wheeling.

Over the years, Edward worked in the Wheeling-Benwood area as a furnace man, laborer, kiln placer, driver, and a steel mill repairman where, in 1939, he earned $713.00 for thirty weeks of work. That same year, Leona assembled toys at a toy factory, earning $652.00 for fifty weeks of work.

After ailing for several months, Edward died at Ohio Valley General Hospital on April 4, 1965. He was a retired driver for Delta Concrete Company and a member of the First Christian Church of Wheeling. Leona died on Christmas Eve 1972 in West Palm Beach, Florida. Both are buried at Holly Memorial Gardens in Colerain, Ohio. Leona purchased that burial plot from her son, John Edward Miller.

AMANDA ELIZABETH HEINLEIN MILLER MORRIS

Amanda Elizabeth Heinlein Miller Morris was the mother of Harry, Minnie, John, and Edward Miller, and the matriarch of the Miller-Morris families. Amanda was born January 22, 1871, in Bellaire, Ohio, the first child of German immigrants Andrew Bartholomew Heinlein and Wilhelmena Christina Hartman Heinlein. She was the daughter-in-law of our immigrant ancestor, John George Miller (Johann Georg Müller) of Germany. Amanda had one brother, Christian Heinlein (nicknamed Heinie), and one sister, Dora Catherine Heinlein Mayhugh.

At age 9, Amanda was attending school in Bellaire, but not much else is known about her until, at age 16, she married Christian Ernest Miller on November 24, 1887, which was the year before the first trolley car began to operate in Wheeling. According to the 1880 U.S. Census, the Miller and Heinlein families lived only a few blocks apart in Bellaire, so their close proximity may be how Amanda and Christian met.

Amanda was a homemaker, and Christian was employed as a laborer. They became the parents of four children: Harry (1889), Minnie (1891), John (1895), and Edward (1897). The family lived in Benwood, West Virginia, at the time of the 1900 U.S. Census. There were two interesting questions on that Census: "Mother of how many children" and "Number of these children living." Amanda's answers were six children and four living. A fifth child, an unnamed female, was born in 1894 but lived only two days. No record of the sixth child was found. Christian died in 1901 leaving Amanda with four children, the youngest being only four years old. Research on what caused Christian's death at age 40 and his exact date of death continues. Records searched for but not found include his death certificate, an obituary, the cemetery record, and the funeral home record. A clue that something was wrong appeared in a tiny news item found in the March 25, 1899, Wheeling Daily Intelligencer: "A benefit supper and dance for Christian Miller will be given at the Drovers Home Hall, April 15." This venue was a mile from the Miller family home in Benwood.

On June 4, 1902, Amanda married her next-door neighbor, Robert Arthur Morris, a widower and father of four children: Archibald, Alta Fay, Nile, and Randall Morris. Robert worked in the plate mill of the National Tube Company, one of several companies that eventually merged to form Wheeling Steel. He was a member of the Modern Woodmen of America.

Their blended families expanded to thirteen children when Amanda and Robert became the parents of five more: Robert, Lillian, Arthur, Virginia, and Laura Morris. Between 1889 and 1911, Amanda gave birth to nine babies who survived.

Amanda Elizabeth had five granddaughters who were given the name Elizabeth in her honor. She didn't want the girls to be named after her because, instead of Elizabeth, they would be called a nickname to distinguish one from the other. Amanda's first husband and her brother were named Christian. A grandson in every generation of descendants has been given that name.

So what happened in Amanda's personal life? Her granddaughters remember eating smearcase (Schmierkäse) at her house. It was a soft cheese, suitable for spreading or eating with a spoon, similar to a sour cottage cheese. Granddaughter Doris said, "It was like a coffeecake with cottage cheese baked and sweetened on top. It was really good."

Amanda was a big woman who could not fit one belt around her ample waist, so she wore two belts connected together as one. She visited her granddaughters Doris, Libby, and Helen at Ohio Valley General Hospital when all of them had their tonsils removed. A plot was purchased in Amanda's name at Rose Hill Cemetery in Bellaire where two of her granddaughters, Anna and Evaline (George Edward's daughters), were buried. Both girls were less than ten months old when they died. Amanda was a member of Wheeling's German Methodist Church. When established in 1839, it was the first "German" church of the Methodist Episcopal Churches built in the world. The original records were written in German.

Amanda's obituary in The Wheeling Register read: "Mrs. Amanda Morris, 58, wife of Robert A. Morris and well-known resident of South Wheeling, died suddenly last night at 6:30 o'clock at the family home, 2847 Eoff Street. Mrs. Morris had partaken of her evening meal with the rest of the members of her family and had gone to her bedroom when she collapsed. Death was said to have been due to a sudden heart attack. Mrs. Morris was a former member of the German Methodist Church."

Amanda died June 23, 1929. The official cause of death was stroke. Three years later, at age 65 and after a long illness, Robert died of myocarditis at home on January 26, 1932.

Amanda and her two husbands were buried at the Miller gravesite in Greenwood Cemetery, Wheeling. When Christian died in 1901, he was buried at Rose Hill Cemetery in Bellaire; but his son, John M. Miller, had the remains transferred to Greenwood Cemetery in October 1947.

John George Miller
and
Metta Wagener Miller

John George Miller (Johann Georg Müller) was our immigrant ancestor who came to America from Germany (Prussia). John's wife was Metta Wagener Miller, and their son Christian Ernest Miller became my great-grandfather. Not a lot is known about them. This is due to a lack of information in public records during their lifetimes and because of their alternate surnames: Müller and Mueller, Wagner and Waggoner.

John George Miller was born October 16, 1831, in Germany (Prussia). It was reported in the 1900 U.S. Census that he immigrated in 1856, although the 1910 U.S. Census reported his arrival as 1846. Confirmation of his last residence in Germany and the actual date he arrived in the U.S. have not been located yet.

On January 13, 1856, John George Miller, a laborer in a rolling (metalworking) mill, married Metta Wagener in Ritchietown (South Wheeling) when Wheeling was still in the Commonwealth of Virginia. They had six children: Mene (1857), Christian (1861), Emma (1865), John (1869), Edna (1874), and Otto (1876). Christian, Emma, and Otto grew to adulthood. Mene died shortly after birth. Their son John was listed in the 1870 and 1880 U.S. Censuses, and Edna was listed in the 1880 U.S. Census. No other records have been found for these two children, and no one seems to know what happened to them. It is noteworthy that family members of later Miller generations were named John and Edna, perhaps in memory of the two children.

Metta Wagener was born in Germany (Hannover). Research showed that a Meta Wagner traveled on the Bremen Ship Admiral from Bremen, Germany, to

Baltimore, arriving in America on November 8, 1853. She emigrated from Polier, Germany, a tiny bump in the road surrounded by farms and mountains. During World War II, this area, which encompasses the region of the Hartz Mountains and the Weser Uplands, was the central training ground for the German Army. The Germans had about 100,000 troops in the area. (Today, we can view Polier on Google Earth.)

A Meta Mueller is listed in the records of Red Men Cemetery, Wheeling. She was born March 8, 1835, and died October 29, 1886. Also buried at that cemetery were twelve people with the surname Wagener or Wagner. Could it be that some of those people were related to our Metta?

After his wife died, John George lived with his daughter, Emma Miller Meyer Suter. He died March 25, 1914, of arteriosclerosis and was buried at Greenwood Cemetery, Wheeling, in an unmarked grave in Section S, Lot 60. The plot was owned by his daughter, Emma, and also became the resting place of Emma and her two husbands. Only the grave of John Meyer (Emma's first husband) has a tombstone; the others are unmarked.

CHRISTIAN ERNEST MILLER

Christian Ernest Miller was born in Virginia in December 1861 before West Virginia was granted US statehood (June 20, 1863). To put this into perspective, earlier in the same year Christian was born, Abraham Lincoln was sworn in as the 16th President of the United States (March 4, 1861), and the Civil War officially began when Confederates fired upon Fort Sumter in Charleston, South Carolina (April 12, 1861).

As mentioned in the section about Amanda Elizabeth Heinlein Miller Morris section, information about Christian is sparse. Most of what we know comes from U.S. Census records and the Wheeling City Directory. Records searched for, but not found, were the death certificate, an obituary, the cemetery record, and the funeral home record.

In his short lifetime, Christian lived in South Wheeling, Bellaire (Ohio), and Benwood (next to South Wheeling). When he was a young man, the Miller and Heinlein families lived only a few blocks from each other in Bellaire. Christian met Amanda Elizabeth Heinlein, and they were married on November 24, 1887, in Belmont County, Ohio.

Christian was a laborer, and Amanda was a homemaker. They were the parents of six children: Harry (1889), Minnie (1891), John (1895), and Edward (1897); all born in Bellaire. Two other unnamed children died in infancy.

According to the 1900 U.S. Census, taken the year before Christian's death, his family lived in Benwood. He died in 1901, leaving Amanda with four small children—the youngest was four years old. We do not know why Christian died at age 40. A clue that something was wrong was a tiny news item (as mentioned earlier) that was found in the March 25, 1899, Wheeling Daily Intelligencer: "A benefit supper and dance for Christian Miller will be given at the Drovers Home Hall, April 15." This venue was a mile from the Miller family home in Benwood.

Christian was buried at Rose Hill Cemetery (Greenwood) in Bellaire. Many years later in October 1947, his son, John M. Miller, had the remains transferred to the Miller gravesite at Greenwood Cemetery in Wheeling.

Christian's youngest grandson, Christian Ernest Miller, was named after him in 1942. Even though Christian's life was short, his given name has lived on in three generations of his grandsons. It is my hope that it will continue in future generations.

About the Author

CAROL J. BELL is a graduate of West Virginia University. She retired after a long career at the Centers for Disease Control and Prevention in Atlanta, Georgia. Her passion has always been genealogy and family history. Carol is a member of the Wheeling Area Genealogical Society and the Daughters of the American Revolution. She lives in Norcross, Georgia, and Wheeling, West Virginia.

www.ingramcontent.com/pod-product-compliance
Lightning Source LLC
Chambersburg PA
CBHW061226150426

42812CB00054BA/2529